THE FLOWER FAIRIES DECOUPAGE BOOK

CICELY MARY BARKER

FREDERICK WARNE

FREDERICK WARNE

Published by The Penguin Group
27 Wrights Lane, London W8 5TZ, England
Penguin Books USA Inc., 375 Hudson Street, New York, New York 10014, USA
Penguin Books Australia Ltd, Ringwood, Victoria, Australia
Penguin Books Canada Ltd, 10 Alcorn Avenue, Toronto, Ontario, Canada M4V 3B2
Penguin Books (NZ) Ltd, 182-190 Wairau Road, Auckland 10, New Zealand

Penguin Books Ltd, Registered Offices:
Harmondsworth, Middlesex, England

First published 1997
1 3 5 7 9 10 8 6 4 2

ISBN 0 7232 4366 2

Colour reproduction by Saxon Photolitho Ltd, Norwich
Printed in Hong Kong by Imago Publishing Ltd.

INTRODUCTION

❋

Snip, snip, snip, go busy fairy scissors,
Pinking out the edges
of the petals of the Pinks!

Cicely Mary Barker was born in Croydon, Surrey on 28 June
1895. She was a devout Christian who used her talent for
painting to express her spiritual beliefs. The first of her Flower Fairies
books was published in 1923 to instant popular acclaim. The public were charmed by her imaginative
vision of a fairy world, in which every tree and flower housed its own guardian fairy. How else were the
petals of the Pinks so delicately fringed but by the nimble hands and scissors of fairies?
She painted from life whenever she could, sometimes enlisting the help of staff at Kew Gardens in
finding and identifying plant specimens. She modelled the fairies on the children who attended her
sister's nursery school. They posed for her in the costumes that she created, and when the paintings
were complete Cicely wrote the accompanying poems.

*   *   *   *

Decoupage comes from the French word meaning 'to cut out', and describes the artform of decorating
objects with printed scraps of paper. Decoupage was most popular in the Victorian era, when a wide
variety of objects, such as screens, photo frames and jewellery boxes were covered over with specially
printed scraps. Decoupage themes such as seaside holidays, angels, children and flowers were
particularly popular.

In this book, you will find a selection of Cicely Mary Barker's exquisite watercolours, each of which is
ideally suited to the romantic tradition of decoupage. There are also 10 suggested projects, complete
with detailed step-by-step instructions on how to achieve a professional and attractive finish.
Decoupage is an inexpensive and creative hobby because it transforms ordinary everyday objects into
beautiful gifts for friends and family.

Materials

❈

You may already have quite a few of the items required for the decoupage projects around the house, but they might have decorated surfaces as part of their design. Spray paint is useful to cover the old design and obtain a smooth plain base colour on which to stick your scraps. These are the basic materials that you will need:

- ❈ brush for varnishing
- ❈ undercoat or primer
- ❈ spray paints
- ❈ P.V.A glue
- ❈ scissors
- ❈ scalpel & cutting mat
- ❈ varnish - satin and gloss finish
- ❈ masking tape

Contents

$\mathcal{H}$ELPFUL $\mathcal{H}$INTS

❋

Most of the projects in this book are simple to make and suitable for beginners. But its worth bearing in mind a few helpful hints to make your decoupage projects as trouble-free as possible.

SPRAY PAINTING

The best place to do this is outside in the garden so that you avoid breathing in any of the fumes or damaging the furnishings. Hold the nozzle about 6 inches from the object and spray with at least two coats to achieve an even finish. Children should not use spray paints - acrylic paints can be used instead.

SCALPEL CARE

To achieve the best results, adults will need to use a scalpel or craft knife to cut around the delicate edges of the scraps. But be careful! Don't hold your fingers next to the blade, and place the scalpel in clear view between uses. When you have finished, stick the blade into a piece of cork.

WARNING!

Children should not use a scalpel or craft knife, but could ask an adult to help them cut around the scraps using a pair of blunt-edged scissors, leaving a small edge around each scrap.

DESIGN

Always position your scraps before sticking them down to achieve the best design. If you do stick a scrap in the wrong place, reposition it immediately, before the glue dries.

CLEANING UP

Always put down plenty of sheets of newspaper when beginning a new decoupage project and don't remove your object until the paint and glue are completely dry. White spirit will remove spray paint and varnish from hands - wash with plenty of warm soapy water afterwards. Brushes should be cleaned with warm soapy water immediately after use.

SEE ABOVE THE FAIRY'S HEAD, GUELDER-ROSE'S BERRIES RED.

ℒetter ℛack

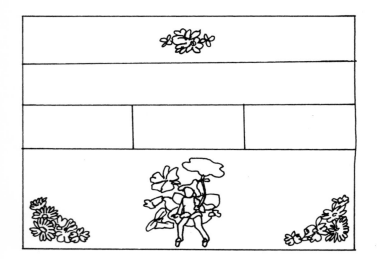

A letter rack is a useful way of organising your correspondence. Our design uses the nasturtium fairy on a black background - the bright orange and black colour scheme shows what a variety of effects you can achieve using the Flower Fairies theme.

You Will Need
a piece of stiff card approx. 75 cm x 50 cm and 2 mm thick ● undercoat or primer ● black spray paint ● scalpel & cutting mat ● double-sided sticky tape ● P.V.A glue ● brush for varnishing ● high gloss varnish

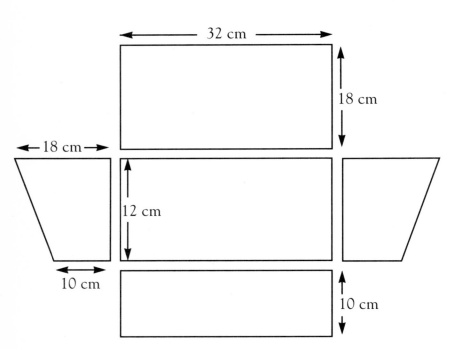

1. Using the scalpel or a sharp pair of scissors, cut panels of card to the required size - follow the diagram for measurements.

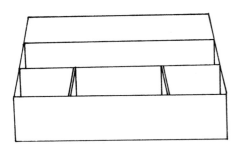

3. Secure the internal panels to make the compartments using double-sided sticky tape. (See diagram).

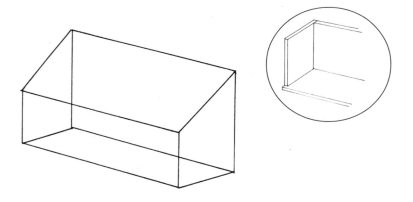

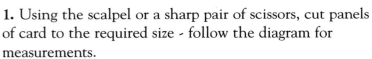

2. Construct the basic shape using double-sided sticky tape along the 2mm edges of the card.
The structure can be strengthened by making the edges butt-up to each other as shown in the diagram circled.

4. Spray the letter rack with an undercoat or primer. Allow to dry, then apply black spray paint.

5. Cut out and arrange your decoupage scraps. Stick them down securely using glue.

6. Apply two coats of high gloss varnish to finish, allowing each coat to dry.

Pencil Holder & Pencils

❁

This pencil holder with matching pencils is an easier project than the letter rack and uses materials you'll probably have around the house. Make your pencil holder and pencils to match the letter rack for a striking set of desk accessories.

You Will Need - for the pencil pot:
a tubular cardboard biscuit or crisp container ● undercoat or primer ● black spray paint ● black paper ● scalpel & cutting mat ● scissors ● P.V.A. glue ● double-sided sticky tape ● brush for varnishing ● high gloss varnish

You Will Need - for the pencils:
black paper ● new pencils ● ruler ● strong glue

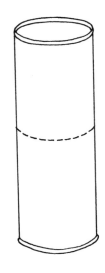

4 Cut out and arrange your scraps (scraps can be temporarily put in place using masking tape). Glue them down securely.

5. Apply two coats of gloss varnish to finish.

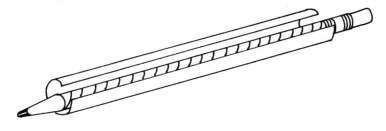

PENCIL POT

1. Cut the biscuit container to approx. 11 cm high. Keep the part with the base.

2. Spray with undercoat. When dry, apply two coats of black spray paint. Remember to spray the inside top edge of the tube.

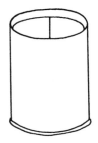

3. Line the inside of the pot with black paper for a neat finish.

PENCILS

1. Measure the length of the pencils and cut a piece of black paper to fit. Wrap it round the pencil and cut off excess paper. Glue down securely.

2. Cut out your decoupage scraps and wrap them around the pencils. Use a strong glue to make them secure.

3. Varnish with a coat of high gloss for a beautiful finish.

$\mathcal{P}$HOTOGRAPH ALBUM

❄

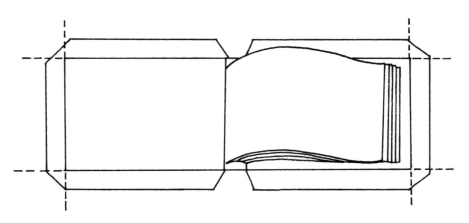

A beautifully decorated album makes a very personal wedding gift and you can decoupage some of the inside pages to provide a pretty frame for special photographs. In the technique described here, two contrasting colours have been used - pink to cover the album and lilac for the spine and endpapers, with a lilac ribbon to match. These colours work well with the pink and lilac flowers of Zinnia, Chicory and Periwinkle.

YOU WILL NEED
a hard-backed photograph album ● pink and lilac coloured paper (enough to cover the album and make the endpapers) ● cream coloured paper ● lilac ribbon (approx. 1/2 metre long) ● scissors ● scalpel & cutting mat P.V.A. glue ● double-sided sticky tape

1. Cover the album: Measure the front of the album. Cut two pieces of lilac paper large enough to cover the front and back of the album, allowing a 3 cm overlap on each of the three sides (not the spine). Stick down using paper glue. Next, using a pair of small scissors, snip the corners diagonally and cut out the corner pieces - follow the dotted lines in the diagram as a guide.

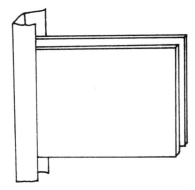

2. Cover the spine: Measure the length and width of the spine. Cut a piece of pink paper to fit, allowing a 3 cm overlap on the width, and about 1/2 cm overlap on the top and bottom of the spine. Make sure that the paper is centrally placed on the spine before sticking it down with glue. Next, using a pair of scissors, cut down the fold lines from the top of the overlap down to the cover of the album. Stick down all edges behind the leaves or pages of the album.
Do the same at each end.

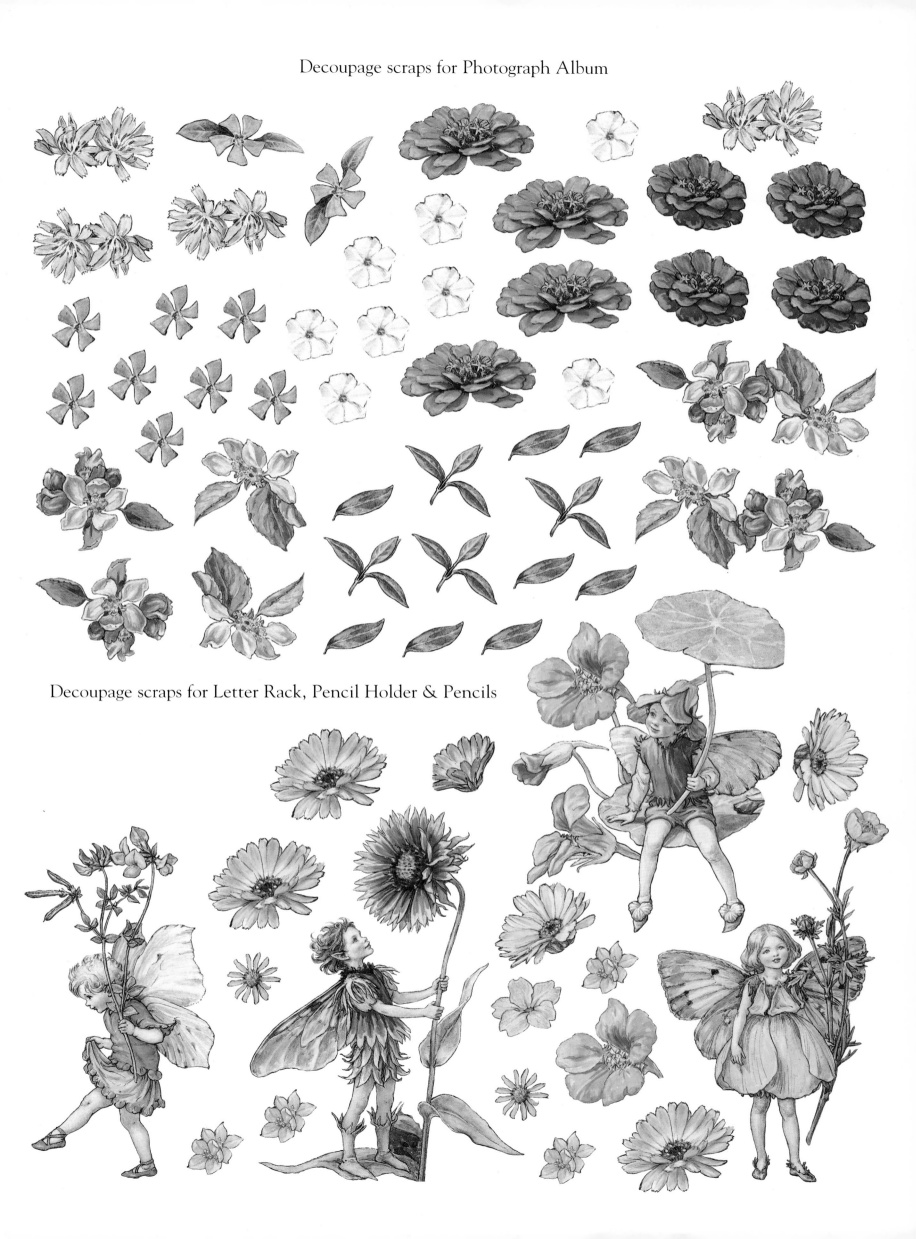

Decoupage scraps for Photograph Album

Decoupage scraps for Letter Rack, Pencil Holder & Pencils

Decoupage scraps for Letter Rack, Pencil Holder & Pencils

Decoupage scraps for Jewellery Box

Decoupage scraps for Lampshade or Fan

Decoupage scraps for Photoframe

Decoupage scraps for Dressing Table Set

Decoupage scraps for Nameplate

Decoupage scraps for Biscuit Tin

Decoupage scraps for Tray

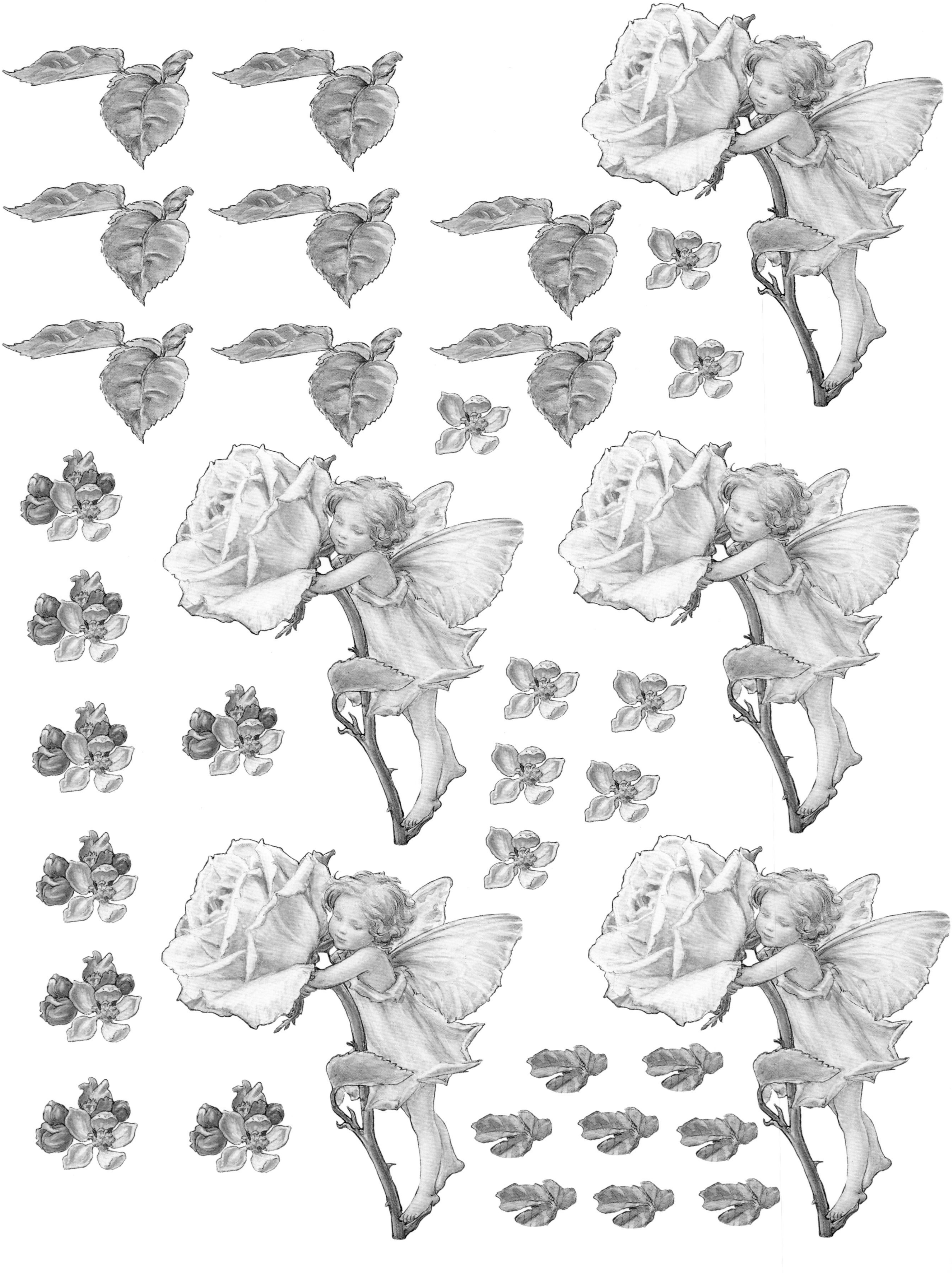

Clockface for Wall Clock

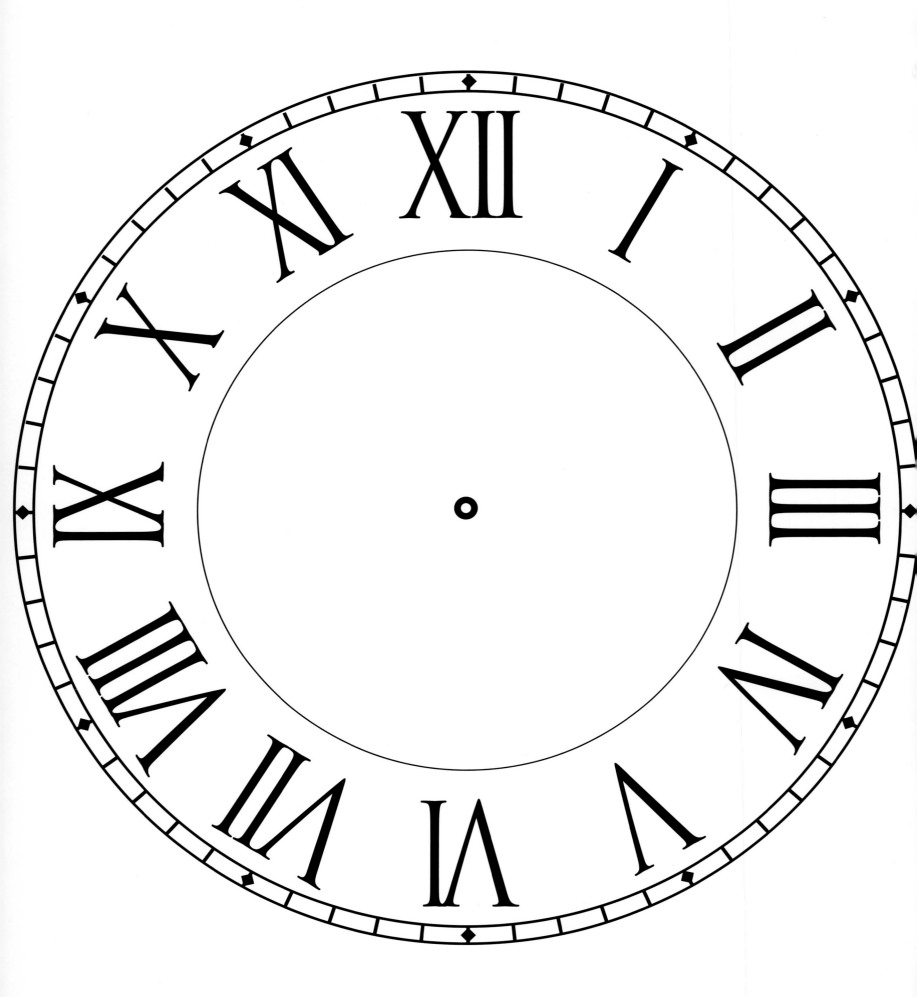

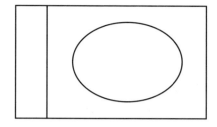

3. Using the white or cream paper, cut out an oval shape large enough to write in. This will give you a central frame on which to decoupage. Practise writing in the words you want in pencil, making sure all the letters fit. When you are happy with it, write on your message in pen and stick the paper down with glue.

4. Cut out your decoupage scraps and arrange your design. When you are happy with it, stick the scraps down securely with glue.

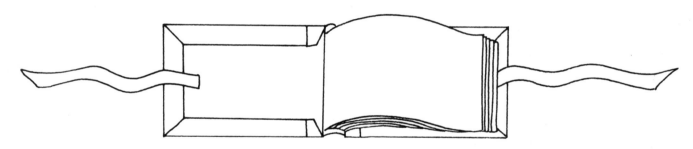

5. Cut the length of ribbon in half. Secure each half to the inside front and back covers, with double-sided sticky tape.

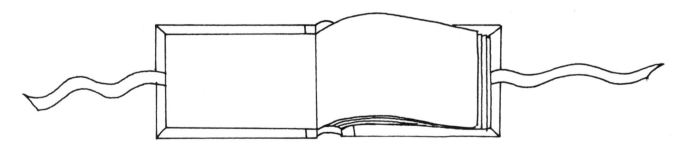

6. Make the endpapers: Measure one of the inside pages of your album and cut two pieces of pink paper in the same size. Stick each piece down to the inside front and back covers. These will cover the edges of the lilac paper and ribbon ends. Stick down with glue.

DRESSING TABLE SET

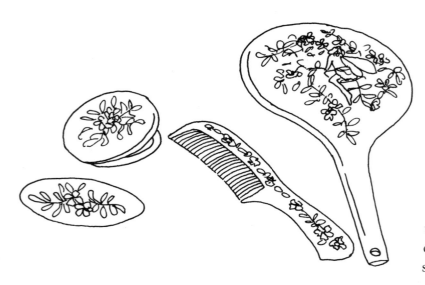

An old-fashioned hand-mirror and a long-handled comb work best for this project - they will be most in keeping with the victorian style. The starry white flowers of the Jasmine Fairy placed against a gold background help create an antique feel to this beautiful dressing table set.

YOU WILL NEED
a long-handled comb ● a hand-mirror ● a powder compact ● a hair clip ● masking tape ● scrap paper ● undercoat or primer ● gold spray paint ● scalpel & cutting mat ● P.V.A. glue ● brush for varnishing ● satin varnish

---

TIP: *Before spraying the mirror or powder compact, make sure you cover the glass with a circle of scrap paper cut to fit, and secured with repositionable glue. Remove the scrap paper when the paint is dry.*

---

1. Apply the undercoat to each item and spray with two coats of gold paint when dry.

2. Decide how many scraps you will use for each item. Cut them out and position them before sticking them down.

3. Apply two coats of satin varnish - this will help secure the scraps down.

MIRROR
Use the Jasmine fairy on the back of the mirror as a centrepiece, then position the flowers around it. Stick some leaf and flower scraps down the handle.

COMB
Alternate the single flowers with the two-leaved scraps along the edge of the comb.

POWDER COMPACT
Position the leaf scraps in the middle of the compact case, so that their stalks are joined at the bottom and their leaves are pointing outwards in a star shape. Then stick a cluster of flowers at the centre, covering the base of the leaf stems.

HAIR CLIP
Position two leaf scraps along the length of the comb, and place some flowers in the centre.

PHOTOFRAME

❋

Making your own photoframe means that you can design a shaped frame to suit a particular photo. This design is easy to create and looks very effective. We have used the pretty Zinnia fairy, whose flower aptly means "Thoughts of absent friends".

YOU WILL NEED
a plain clipframe ● thick card larger than the clipframe and approx. 4 mm thick ● a pencil ● undercoat or primer ● black spray paint ● scalpel & cutting mat ● paper glue ● strong glue ● double-sided sticky tape ● high gloss varnish

1. Measure your clipframe. Draw the shape of your frame on the card with a pencil (remember to allow a 1 cm overlap on the inner frame). Cut it out.

2. Spray the card frame with undercoat. When dry, apply two coats of black spray paint.

3. Cut out your decoupage scraps and stick them onto the card frame. In our design, the fairy and some of the flowers overlap the inner and outer edges of the frame. Glue scraps firmly in place and varnish with a high gloss finish - this will help stiffen the overlapping pieces.

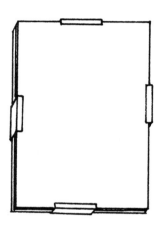

4. Place your picture or photograph in the clipframe. Attach the cardboard frame to the clipframe using double-sided sticky tape.

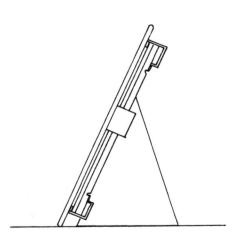

5. To stand the frame upright on a desk or table, cut out a rectangular piece of card. Fold it in half diagonally, and stick one half to the back of the frame.

LAMPSHADE

❋

The Cornflower and Red Clover Fairies look charming on this easy-to-make decoupaged lampshade, especially when lit from underneath. Its ideal for a child's bedroom - a little varnish helps keep the fairies in place but don't use spray paint (it isn't safe).

YOU WILL NEED
a plain pale-coloured lampshade ● scalpel & cutting mat ● P.V.A. glue ● brush for varnishing ● satin varnish

1. Cut out your decoupage scraps and stick them onto the lampshade using glue. In our design we have alternated the blue Cornflower Fairy with the Red Clover Fairy, using the flower scraps as a divide. The small leaf scraps look good positioned around the top rim of the shade.

2. Brush on a coat of varnish. Allow to dry and repeat.

DECORATIVE FAN

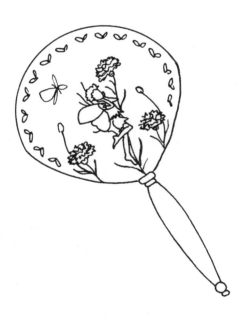

This decorative fan is intended as an alternative project to the lampshade, using the same scraps. It is simple to make and is a really beautiful item to display on the mantlepiece.

YOU WILL NEED
a flat fan ● masking tape ● cream and blue spray paint (to match the Cornflower Fairy) ● scalpel & cutting mat ● P.V.A. glue ● brush for varnishing ● satin varnish

1. Spray the fan with undercoat. When dry, cover the handle with scrap paper secured with masking tape. Spray the fan with cream spray paint.

2. When dry, cover the fan with scrap paper. Apply two coats of blue spray paint to the handle.

3. Cut out your decoupage scraps and position them on the fan. Stick them down with glue.

4. Brush on a coat of satin varnish. Allow to dry and repeat.

NAMEPLATE

❋

This nameplate is one of the most simple projects to make. We have used the Strawberry Fairy whose bright red and green colours will be popular with every child who receives the nameplate as a gift. Try to use rub-down letters that will be in keeping with the design you use.

YOU WILL NEED
thick card or foam board approx. 4mm thick ● ¹/2 metre of wired red ribbon ● P.V.A. glue ● undercoat or primer ● cream spray paint ● scalpel & cutting mat ● brush for varnishing ● satin varnish ● double-sided sticky tape ● rub down letters

1. In pencil, write out the name or words on the foam board. Design a shape around it, and cut out.

2. Spray with undercoat. When dry, apply the cream spray paint.

3. Cut out your decoupage scraps and arrange your design around the name. Stick down the scraps securely with glue.

4. Rub down the letters. If you make a mistake in positioning, you should be able to scrape off the letters using a scalpel.

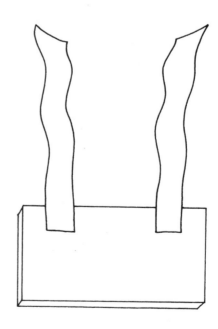

5. Cut ribbon in half. Secure each end with double-sided sticky tape to the underside of the nameplate. Tie the loose ends together in a pretty bow and hang.

Jewellery Box

❋

This beautiful box is a perfect place to keep pretty sea shells, scented soaps, pot pourri or jewellery. We have used the Periwinkle Fairy as the focus, agreeing with the poem that Cicely Mary Barker wrote of this fairy - "Who does not love Periwinkle's blue?". Make a separate shelf for your rings and line the box with felt for the finishing touch.

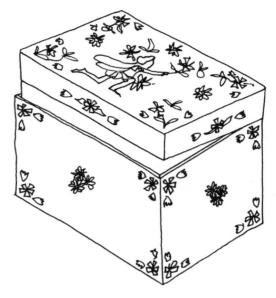

YOU WILL NEED
a hinged box ● stiff card approx. 2 mm thick ● undercoat or primer ●powder blue spray paint ● scalpel & cutting mat ● P.V.A. glue ● double-sided sticky tape ●brush for varnishing ●high gloss varnish ●felt to line the box and tray

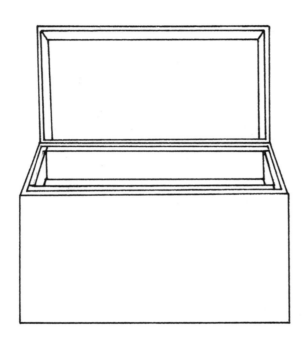

1. Spray the box with undercoat. When dry, apply two coats of blue spray paint.

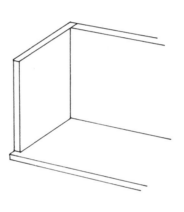

> **TIP** *The structure can be strengthened by making the edges butt-up to each other as shown in the diagram.*

2. Measure the inside length and width of the box. Cut out the panels for the tray as above, to fit the size of your box. Construct the basic shape using double-sided sticky tape along the 2mm edges of the card.

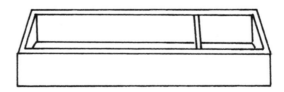

3. Spray the outside of the tray to match the box.

4. Cut out and arrange your decoupage scraps and stick them down using P.V.A. Cover with two coats of high gloss varnish.

5. Line the inside of the box and tray with felt, stuck down with glue.

$\mathcal{W}$ALL $\mathcal{C}$LOCK

This charming wall clock would make a delightful gift for anyone and isn't difficult to create. You should be able to find the clock mechanism in most good arts and craft shops, and in watchmaker's and jewellers.

YOU WILL NEED
battery-operated clock mechanism and clock hands ● a piece of thick card or plywood large enough to fit on the clockface and scraps ● undercoat or primer ● cream spray paint ● compasses ● P.V.A glue ● ruler ● pencil ● scalpel & cutting mat ● brush for varnishing ● satin varnish

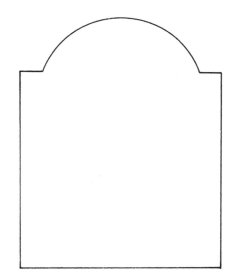

1. Design your clock shape, allowing enough space for the clock face supplied, and for placing scraps around the edges and top. Cut it out and spray with undercoat. Allow to dry, then apply two coats of cream spray paint.

3. Cut out your decoupage scraps and arrange them around the clock face. We have used the Apple Blossom Fairy as the main top decoration, with blossom positioned around the corners and centre of the face. Stick the scraps down securely. You can make a border from coloured paper.

5. Attach the clock mechanism and hands.

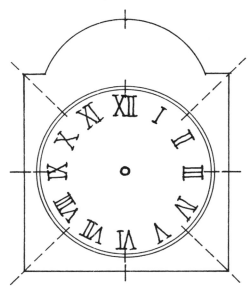

2. Cut out the clock face and place it onto your clock shape, making sure that it is positioned centrally by taking measurements from the edges with a ruler. When you are happy with the positioning, hold in place, lift one side and glue firmly. Repeat on the other side. Make a hole in the centre for the clock mechanism.

BISCUIT TIN AND TRAY

❁

The Narcissus and Lavender Fairies have been selected to decorate the tin, with one of Cicely Mary Barker's most exquisite watercolours - the Rose Fairy - on the tea tray. This tea-set is one of the simplest projects to decorate, but don't just bring it out for afternoon tea - put it on display in the kitchen or dining-room.

YOU WILL NEED
biscuit tin ● wooden or tin tray ● scrap paper ● masking tape ● undercoat or primer ● dark green spray paint ● scalpel & cutting mat ● brush for varnishing ● high gloss varnish

1. Spray the tray and tin with undercoat - Cover the inside of the tin with scrap paper attached with masking tape and make sure you spray the tin and lid separately. When dry, apply a coat of dark green spray paint.

2. Cut out and position your decoupage scraps - do not use masking tape as it may remove the spray paint. Stick them down securely.

3. Brush on three coats of varnish, allowing each coat to dry.

❁